The Road to Success:

An Orientation Process for Catholic School Teachers

Jim Brennan, Ed.D.

**Department of Elementary Schools
National Catholic Educational Association**

copyright©1995 by the National Catholic Educational Association, Washington, D.C.
All rights reserved, including the right of reproducing in whole or part in any form.
Published in the United States of America by the National Catholic Educational Association.
ISBN # 1-55833-149-2

Table of Contents

PREFACE iii
ABOUT THE AUTHOR iv
TO THE PRINCIPAL: v
    Orientation v
    New Teachers and Experienced Teachers vi
    Participants vi
        The principal's role vi
        The experienced (buddy) teacher's role vii
        The new teacher's role vii
    Program Topics vii
    Program Design viii
    Orientation Timeline ix
    Orientation Design x
    Getting Started xi
    Program Initiation xii
    Closure xii
    Teacher Orientation Competencies Record xiii

INTRODUCTION 1
    The Teacher in the Catholic School 1
    The Program 2

CHAPTER ONE - FINDING YOUR WAY 3
    Worksheet   1 - 1   Orientation to School Personnel 6
    Worksheet   1 - 2   School Resources 7
    Worksheet   1 - 3   Diocesan Resource Personnel 8
    Worksheet   1 - 4   Paper Work 9
    Worksheet   1 - 5   Schedules and Policies 10
    Worksheet   1 - 6   School Equipment 11
    Worksheet   1 - 7   Noninstructional Duties 12
    Worksheet   1 - 8   Personnel Policies 13
    Worksheet   1 - 9   Public Resources 14
    Worksheet   1 - 10   School Places 15
    Worksheet   1 - 11   The Local Community 16

CHAPTER TWO - CREATING THE CLASSROOM CLIMATE 17
    Worksheet   2 - 1   Philosophy 20
    Worksheet   2 - 2   Religious Practices 21
    Worksheet   2 - 3   The Classroom 22
    Worksheet   2 - 4   Classroom Management 24
    Worksheet   2 - 5   Classroom Procedures 25
    Worksheet   2 - 6   Classroom Energy 26
    Worksheet   2 - 7   The First Day of School 27

CHAPTER THREE - PLANNING MEANINGFUL LESSONS 29
    Six-Step Lesson Plan 30
    Instructional Strategies 31
    A Strategy for Incorporating a Value into a Lesson 33
    Worksheet   3 - 1   Lesson Design Planning Sheet 34
    Worksheet   3 - 2   Lesson Plan Review 35
    Worksheet   3 - 3   Curriculum 36

CHAPTER FOUR - SUPPORT 37
    Worksheet   4 - 1   Faculty Who Can Help 39
    Worksheet   4 - 2   Plan for Success 40
    Worksheet   4 - 3   Plan for Success: Action Plan 41

CHAPTER FIVE - TEACHER'S PROFESSIONAL JOURNAL 43
    Worksheet   5 - 1   Teacher's Professional Journal 45

COMPUTER SPECIFICATIONS 52

Preface

Our Catholic school teachers are the most valuable resource in our schools. Therefore, every effort must be made to acquaint them with the purpose and mission of our schools and to assist them to perfect their instructional techniques. The orientation of teachers to Catholic schools provides the opportunity to gradually introduce teachers into this community of educators.

Dr. Jim Brennan, a principal from the Diocese of Oakland, wisely entitled his work *The Road to Success: An Orientation Process for Catholic School Teachers* which suggests that the orientation is not limited to one day or a short space of time but rather it stretches out over time and its purpose is to assist new teachers to function effectively in this community of believing educators. The orientation process is not an end in itself; it is a means to enable teachers to be successful. When teachers are successful, the students are the primary beneficiaries.

Another feature of this process is that it is interactive. The orientation doesn't consist of just giving teachers information and hoping they will digest all the new data. This process calls for a new teacher to discover the information and reflect on it under the guidance of the principal and a buddy teacher. This team of three frequently comes together during the orientation period to share experiences and insights. The new teacher has a support group. The journaling process that the program calls for encourages the new teacher to reflect on what was learned and to internalize it.

The NCEA Department of Elementary Schools expresses its gratitude to Jim Brennan for sharing his process with the entire Catholic school community. The Department offers this process to its member schools with the hope that this will enable many new teachers to have successful teaching careers in Catholic schools.

Mary Ann Governal, OSF, Ed.D. *Robert J. Kealey, Ed.D.*
President *Executive Director*

Feast of
St. Joseph, Mentor of Jesus, 1995

About the Author

Dr. Brennan is a native of Chicago. He received his bachelor's degree from Loras College in Dubuque, Iowa, and his master's degree from Chicago State University. In 1979 upon moving to the San Francisco area, he began graduate work at the University of San Francisco. In 1983 he received his doctorate in organization and leadership from the School of Education at USF.

Since 1969 Dr. Brennan has worked in the ministry of Catholic education in the Archdiocese of Chicago and the Diocese of Oakland. He has served as a teacher and administrator at the elementary school, secondary school, and collegiate levels of education. Currently Dr. Brennan is principal of Holy Spirit School (Pre-K - 8) in Fremont, California, and serves as an adjunct professor in the School of Education at St. Mary's College in Moraga, California.

Dr. Brennan is a member of the Board of Directors of the Fremont Chamber of Commerce. In 1992 he completed the National Catholic Educational Association Principals Academy. In 1993 he was elected by his peers to the NCEA Department of Elementary Schools Executive Committee to represent all the Catholic elementary schools on the Pacific coast.

In honor of his 25th year in Catholic education, he was awarded the Presidential Award from NCEA during Catholic Schools Week.

To the Principal

This section serves as a guide and resource for principals who will utilize the program *The Road to Success: An Orientation Process for Catholic School Teachers*. The program is intended to assist principals as they facilitate the effective inclusion of new teachers into their school community. It provides a framework which principals will need to personalize to their particular school before beginning this orientation program.

Principals may find it helpful to have read the other chapters before proceeding through this section. The details and forms that are explained in the subsequent chapters will be referred to in this section and utilized as the program unfolds.

Orientation

The orientation program presented in this book is a dynamic one that should more accurately be referred to as a process: a process that requires the new teacher to discover the needed information to become an effective teacher in this school. This process involves the new teacher in ongoing experiences that seek to promote understanding and success. This is not a program of merely filling out forms, rather it calls for the teacher to record, reflect, and discuss his/her initial orientation experiences in order to build long-term success. The identified activities call for action and involvement on the part of the new teacher. This is accomplished and enhanced through the guidance of the principal and an identified experienced teacher or buddy teacher.

The principal schedules the initial few meetings with the new teacher and buddy teacher. At the initial meeting the principal explains the process to the new teacher and introduces him or her to the buddy teacher. The principal gives the new teacher and the buddy teacher a copy of this program and a schedule that will be followed regarding the program and the follow-up conferences. Once the first few meetings are completed and the new teacher has gained some sense of direction, it becomes the new teacher's responsibility to schedule a series of meetings with the principal and the buddy teacher for the completion of this program. These meetings will prove successful only if all involved are committed to carrying out the process. These meetings are held very frequently at first, meeting once a day for the first two weeks, but taper off as the necessary information is acquired and a rapport is built among participants. These meetings can be long or very short depending on the needs of the new teacher. The topics listed in the timeline should be covered, but there should also be a flexibility to adjust to a particular need of the new teacher.

A significant component of the process is that the information and involvement that is requested from the new teacher is recorded in a professional journal. Many different forms are suggested in this book which cover specific areas of information needed for the new teacher to adjust to the new school. These forms have a single focus and a simple format making them easy to complete. All the forms in this program can be used as they are presented in the book, or revised to fit local specifications. Any revision can be readily accomplished since the worksheets are available on computer disk. The text is available on Microsoft Word 3.0 for the Macintosh, IBM WordPerfect 5.1 or in an Asci text file.

The fact that the forms are also provided on a computer disk not only makes revisions easily accomplished, but also the entire process can be recorded on a computer eliminating the need for additional pieces of paper. The intent of the program is that the focus can be on the process of what is to be accomplished and not on the paper work.

New Teachers and Experienced Teachers

This program is designed for teachers new to the profession. It can also be used, however, to meet the needs of the experienced teacher transitioning to a new school. Although needs will vary with each teacher, content items listed in this chapter under Orientation Design marked with asterisks should be considered as the primary focus for the experienced teacher. Because of the streamlining of the content for the experienced teacher, the intensity of meetings may be lessened but the number of meetings should continue until the end of the first semester.

Participants

The participants and their identified roles are explained below. The principal should read and review these in order to make any necessary changes before communicating these roles to those involved in the process. In addition to the principal and new teacher, the program calls for an experienced (buddy) teacher. While Catholic school faculties are generally not so large that there would be an abundance of teachers to play the role of buddy teacher, this selection is a crucial decision for the principal to ensure the success of the program and the development of the new teacher.

The buddy teacher should be a post-probationary teacher who has a position that will be impacted by the new teacher. If the new teacher is a second grade teacher, then perhaps the third grade teacher might have a vested interest in the success of the new teacher, especially if these two grades share some common projects. If there are two or more teachers on the same grade level, perhaps one of these could serve as the buddy teacher. Typically, Catholic school teachers are more than willing to help the newcomer to their community. The principal chooses and prepares a buddy teacher who will enthusiastically work with the new teacher in this program.

Since this program is focused on building relationships, from its beginning each person needs a clear understanding of the expectations and responsibilities of all those involved in the process. The roles and responsibilities of the primary participants are outlined below.

The principal's role

In the orientation process the principal's responsibilities are:

1. To demonstrate an active interest and support for the new teacher, and to be available for regular consultation

2. To select an experienced teacher who is qualified and willing to accept the responsibility of working closely with the new teacher

3. To retain the ultimate responsibility for the evaluation of the new teacher

4. To familiarize the new teacher with the ethnic and socioeconomic composition of the community

5. To share the philosophy of the school with the new teacher

6. To make provisions as far as is reasonably possible and appropriate for the new teacher to observe and be observed by teachers of similar grade/subject areas

7. To meet with the new teacher at a regularly scheduled time during the new teacher's orientation period

8. To evaluate periodically the progress of the new teacher with input from the buddy teacher

The experienced (buddy) teacher's role
In this orientation process, the responsibilities of the buddy teacher are:

1. To assist the new teacher during the initial year in the school

2. To offer enthusiastic encouragement and support to the new teacher

3. To be a resource person, especially in the areas of instructional strategies and classroom management

4. To meet with the new teacher at regularly scheduled times during the new teacher's orientation period

5. To participate in conferences with the new teacher and the principal

The new teacher's role
In the orientation process, the responsibilities of the new teacher are:

1. To be willing to accept the advice and counsel of the buddy teacher and the principal

2. To respect the value of professional supervision and evaluation

3. To observe and record the teaching techniques of other experienced teachers in order to improve one's own style

4. To involve oneself in the life of the school

5. To facilitate the regular schedule of meetings with the principal and buddy teacher

6. To contribute actively to these meetings and record appropriate information for future reference and use

Program Topics

In addition to the people involved, there needs to be a focus or direction to the orientation process. The following outline suggests topics to emphasize. Principals should feel free to add other topics to the list as the local situation warrants. Some of these topics have supporting journal forms in the subsequent chapters and some are identified without supportive forms. All of the listed topics can be discussed in the orientation process and recorded in the new teacher's professional journal.

Major topics to review during the orientation program are:

1. **Philosophy:** understanding and support of the principles and practices of Catholic education and the school

2. **Documents:** establishing familiarity with existing arch/diocesan or school documents, curricular guides or courses of study

3. **Curriculum:** learning what is to be taught and establishing long-term and intermediate objectives for these learning objectives within the overall curriculum plan of the school

4. **Lesson Planning:** preparing topics with appropriate strategies for immediate objectives

5. **Strategies:** becoming aware of a variety of instructional strategies for diverse situations

6. **Organization:** obtaining understanding and appropriate use of grouping and regrouping for instruction

7. **Pupil Evaluation:** using and understanding a variety of assessment techniques

8. **Pupil Management:** developing appropriate behavior expectations and consequences

9. **Relationships:** developing a rapport with students, faculty, staff, parents, and community;

10. **Operational Responsibilities:** understanding of non-instructional duties

Program Design

The design that follows gives the principal an indication of timeline and content that are part of the process. In addition to the orientation topics identified, a general timeline is presented below. Although this timeline calls for a substantial amount of the principal's time at a very busy part of the year, this time is time well spent. The schedule commits the principal to a significant amount of time with the new teacher at the beginning of the school year when the new teacher is most in need of this special attention and the chances for failure are greatest.

The timeline provided, however, is meant only as a starting point. The principal has the responsibility to identify clearly the timeline and content that will be followed during the orientation process for this individual teacher. A flexible schedule will best meet each participant's needs.

The principal, buddy teacher, and new teacher need to refer regularly to the major topics listed above. All of these topics need to be covered during the period of orientation. While the general tenor of the program calls for these topics to be addressed as the need arises, the suggested timeline illustrates how the program can evolve. The connection between the chart listing the orientation timeline and the chart listing the orientation design is identified through the numbers listed in the left hand column of each chart. The numbers correlate what should be covered with when it should be covered.

Orientation Timeline

No.	Phase	Activity	Timeline	Facilitator
1	Hiring	Job offer	May 1st	Principal
2	Initial Induction	Contract Documents Manuals	May 15th	Principal
2	Preparation for new year	Principal/ Teacher Conf.	Aug. 1st	Principal
2	Continued preparation	Buddy/New Teacher Conf.	Aug. 15th	Buddy Teacher
3	Beginning	Principal/ New Teacher Conf.	Daily 1st two weeks	New Teacher
3	Beginning	Buddy Teacher/ New Teacher Conf.	Daily 1st two weeks	New Teacher
4	Continuing	Principal/ New Teacher Conf.	Weekly 1st quarter	New Teacher
4	Continuing	Buddy Teacher/ New Teacher Conf.	Weekly 1st quarter	New Teacher
5	Supporting	Principal/ New Teacher Conf.	Bi-weekly 1st semester	New Teacher
5	Supporting	Buddy Teacher/ New Teacher	Bi-weekly 1st semester	New Conf. Teacher
6	Ongoing	Principal/ New Teacher Conf.	As needed	New Teacher
6	Ongoing	Buddy Teacher/ New Teacher Conf.	As needed	New Teacher

Orientation Design

No.	Phase	Topic	Worksheet Form
1	Initial	Philosophy*	2-1
		Religious Practices	2-2
2	Prior to School Opening	School Personnel *	1-1
		School Places*	1-10
		The Classroom	2-3
		Local Community	1-11
		Classroom Procedures	2-5
		The First Day of School*	2-7
		Curriculum	3-3
		Six-Step Plan	
		Instructional Strategies	
		Lesson Design*	3-1
		Professional Journal*	5-1
3	First Two Weeks	School Resources*	1-2
		Paper Work*	1-4
		Schedules and Policies*	1-5
		School Equipment*	1-6
		Lesson Design	3-1
		Lesson Review*	3-2
		Professional Journal*	5-1
4	First Quarter	Diocesan Resources	1-3
		Classroom Management	2-4
		Six-Step Plan	
		Instructional Strategies	
		Lesson Design	3-1
		Lesson Review	3-2
		Professional Journal*	5-1
		A Strategy for Integrating a Value into a Lesson	
5	Second Quarter	Public Resources*	1-9
		Classroom Energy	2-6
		Lesson Review	3-2
		Planning for Success*	4-2
		Professional Journal*	5-1
6	Second Semester	Review as needed*	
		Conference Log*	5-1

* Indicates areas of concentration for an experienced teacher's orientation.

Getting Started

Having presented the background of the program, its focus, and an understanding of what kind of a schedule it requires, use of the materials will now be addressed.

The body of this book is divided into five chapters.

1. **Finding Your Way**
   This chapter calls for the new teacher to identify significant members of both the local and the broader school community and to secure information from the learning community.

2. **Creating the Classroom Climate**
   This chapter provides opportunities for the new teacher to surface and discuss techniques and methods to create a dynamic place for children to learn in the classroom.

3. **Planning Meaningful Lessons**
   This chapter challenges the new teacher to identify methodologies and test them to see which methodologies best suit the abilities of the teacher and the needs of the students.

4. **Support**
   This chapter calls for the new teacher to identify all the resources for professional growth, and to realize that he/she is not alone, but part of a learning community.

5. **Teacher's Professional Journal**
   The last chapter provides and encourages the new teacher to use the forms to create a reflective journal to promote professional growth and serve as a reference for future reflections.

First, the principal needs to browse through the other parts of this book and become familiar with the content of the process. The chapters of the book are not meant to be discrete entities, but rather interrelated components. Through necessity more than one chapter may be focused on at a time.

The sections include worksheets that need to be filled in with appropriate information. The new teacher needs to find the information that is requested. This self-learning deepens one's understanding of the expected knowledge. During the meetings with the principal and/or the buddy teacher, the information is reviewed and, hopefully, serves as a catalyst for discussion regarding the whys and/or hows of a particular situation.

The researched and discussed information is recorded on the worksheets provided and the completed worksheets are placed in a notebook, or on a computer, so that the new teacher has a quick and easy point of reference when information is needed. Having researched, recorded, and discussed the information, the new teacher will have enhanced his/her ability to find, recall, and utilize the necessary facts. The intent here is not merely factual identification or memorization, but an in-depth understanding which leads to clearer and stronger implementation.

The completed and discussed forms should be kept by the teacher. The principal needs only to retain in the teacher's permanent file the Teacher Orientation Competencies Record for documentation of the orientation process.

Program Initiation

The initiation of this program rests with the principal. Once the new teacher has been hired and the buddy teacher engaged, it is up to the principal to get things going. This entails reviewing the program with the new teacher and the buddy teacher, seeing they have copies of the program, and setting a starting date and an action plan for implementation.

The principal needs to schedule some three-way meetings (principal, new teacher, and buddy teacher) to enable the principal to do a perception check on the working relationship of the new teacher and the buddy teacher, and to do some informal needs assessment regarding the future direction of the program.

Closure

Although the timeline calls for the majority of orientation topics to be covered during the first semester, at times it may be necessary to continue the process through the second semester. The orientation process will be concluded once the new teacher has completed at least one semester of teaching at the school and has indicated achievement of the competencies listed on the form below. This form, when it is completed, could be inserted into the new teacher's personnel file as documentation for the orientation process.

TEACHER ORIENTATION COMPETENCIES RECORD

_____ has demonstrated knowledge and understanding of the information contained on the worksheets listed below. The initials of the new teacher, buddy teacher and/or principal attest to this.

	New Teacher	Buddy Teacher or Principal	Date
1. Orientation to School Personnel, 1 - 1	____	____	____
2. School Resources, 1 - 2	____	____	____
3. Diocesan Resource Personnel, 1 - 3	____	____	____
4. Paper Work, 1 - 4	____	____	____
5. Schedules and Policies, 1 - 5	____	____	____
6. School Equipment, 1 - 6	____	____	____
7. Noninstructional Duties, 1 - 7	____	____	____
8. Personnel Policies, 1 - 8	____	____	____
9. Public Resources, 1 - 9	____	____	____
10. School Places, 1 - 10	____	____	____
11. The Local Community, 1 - 11	____	____	____
12. Philosophy, 2 - 1	____	____	____
13. Religious Practices, 2 - 2	____	____	____
14. The Classroom, 2 - 3	____	____	____
15. Classroom Management, 2 - 4	____	____	____
16. Classroom Procedures, 2 - 5	____	____	____
17. Classroom Energy, 2 - 6	____	____	____
18. The First Day of School, 2 - 7	____	____	____
19. Lesson Design Planning Sheet, 3 - 1	____	____	____

	New Teacher	Buddy Teacher or Principal	Date
20. Lesson Plan Review, 3 - 2	_____	_____	_____
21. Curriculum, 3 - 3	_____	_____	
21. Faculty Who Can Help, 4 - 1	_____	_____	_____
22. Plan for Success, 4 - 2	_____	_____	_____
23. Plan for Success: Action Plan, 4 - 3	_____	_____	_____
24. Teacher's Professional Journal, 5 - 1	_____	_____	_____

_____ _____ _____ _____
Date of Completion　　New Teacher　　Buddy Teacher　　Principal

Introduction

The Teacher in the Catholic School

Welcome to the Catholic school community!

The Catholic community calls upon Catholic schools to provide a quality Catholic education for their children. These schools are called to become American Catholic schools for the 21st Century which champion superior standards of academic excellence, and integrate gospel values and Catholic Church teaching in the lives and work of all members of the school community. Catholic schools open their minds and hearts and doors to an increasingly diverse world, and prepare their students' minds, hearts and hands to live wisely and generously in a technologically complex and interdependent world. The teacher bears the primary responsibility for this. The teacher as a faith-filled person willingly responds to the challenge to teach as Jesus did, that is, to spread the message of the good news, to build community in which the Eucharist is the highest form of celebration, and to be of service to others. The Catholic school seeks to permeate every educational experience with the message of love and the vitality of Christ's presence; therefore, the message of Jesus needs to be an integral part of all that happens in the school.

The American Catholic bishops in 1972 in their pastoral letter *To Teach as Jesus Did* clearly stated the importance of Catholic schools when they wrote, "Of the educational programs available to the Catholic community, Catholic schools afford the fullest and best opportunity to realize the threefold purpose of Christian education among children and young people." Teaching in a Catholic school is raised to a ministry of the church. The Catholic community, therefore, must ensure that those who engage in it exercise this ministry in a most professional and prayerful manner.

Principals and administrators in Catholic schools have the responsibility to see that those who have been hired to teach are enabled to do so effectively. **The Road to Success: An Orientation Process for Catholic School Teachers** addresses the orientation of the Catholic school teacher from an educational perspective. Other NCEA publications and programs focus on the spiritual formation of the teacher.

Teaching in any school can be a most formidable task. In a Catholic school this is perhaps even more challenging because the spiritual formation of the students is integrated with their academic, social, and physical development. The following pages set forth a process which will assist you, the teacher new to this Catholic school, to carry out your academic duties as a foundation for ministering to the students of the school.

The Program

This book is a living document for you, the new teacher. For you, jointly with your buddy or experienced teacher, and your principal, it serves as a record and a support for your orientation to this school. The worksheets are provided in both print and computer disk format, IBM WordPerfect 5.1 or Macintosh MicroSoft Works 3.0. If you are using the computer disk format, you may more easily adapt the program to meet your needs. The computer disk format allows you, the user, to change some of the forms before they are printed, or perhaps not to print them at all but to store all the information in the memory of the computer. You and your team of educators could feasibly work entirely on the computer and not need to add another sheet of paper to your lives!

To understand how to use *The Road to Success: An Orientation Process for Catholic School Teachers*, it is important that you comprehend and appreciate the philosophy regarding orientation that is central to this process. Orientation is viewed not as a one-time or short-term process, but as an ongoing process designed to enhance the long term success of the new teacher. This orientation process provides a gradual sharing of information and ongoing opportunities to question, exchange ideas, and receive feedback from the many people who become part of your orientation process.

The actual schedule of activities will vary from situation to situation because each teacher is different, and teachers' hiring dates, due to a variety of factors, occur at many different times in the year. How do you use this program? You, the new teacher, and the principal set up a schedule of meetings with identified topics to be addressed at each meeting. This plan addresses your needs, includes all the information to which you need to be introduced and provides the opportunity for the principal to share his/her expectations of you.

Your principal will assign to you a buddy teacher. This teacher has several years of teaching experience. The principal has selected this teacher because the principal has high regard for him or her. Your buddy teacher has agreed to assist you and is most willing to help you. You, your buddy teacher and the principal will work as a team over the next several months. Feel free to call upon their wealth of experience.

This book/program/process is not an end in itself; it is a catalyst for a positive working relationship and an opportunity for growth for you, the buddy teacher and the principal. The various forms found in the following chapters should be adapted to your local situation and then completed either by writing, typing, or utilizing the computer. Because of the amount of new information you need to assimilate, the completed forms serve as a reference for future use and reinforcement.

You may wish to read the section entitled "To the Principal" which provides a detailed overview of the program and shows how the principal will direct this process.

Much success with this program and with your teaching career!

1

Finding Your Way

Finding Your Way

One of your first challenges as a teacher coming into a new school is to find your way around and learn how to get things done. Of course, this includes learning the names, titles, and functions of those with whom you will need to interact within the school building, the parish, and in the larger community. Learning who these individuals are and what they do will open doors to learning many of the procedures necessary for you as you begin your teaching ministry in this school.

The worksheets provided in this first chapter seek very basic information, yet very important data for you. This initial knowledge of people and processes leads to long-term success. These worksheets are completed by you at the beginning of the school year. The schedule developed by the principal may follow the model set forth in the section in this book entitled "To the Principal." When you complete each of these sheets, the content should be discussed in a conference with the principal and/or the buddy teacher, and the discussion summarized by you in your teacher's professional journal which is discussed in Chapter 5. When the worksheets are discussed, they should be signed by the parties involved. You should keep the completed worksheets either in this book or in a binder so you will have them for future reference.

This chapter includes the following worksheets.

Worksheet 1 - 1 Orientation to School Personnel
This worksheet requires you to record the names of the key administrative personnel at the school.

Worksheet 1 - 2 School Resources
This second worksheet asks you to identify the names of key parent and community resources at the school.

Worksheet 1 - 3 Diocesan Resource Personnel
This worksheet informs you of the resources available through the local arch/diocese.

Worksheet 1 - 4 Paper Work
This worksheet asks you to research the required paper work procedures at this school.

Worksheet 1 - 5 Schedules and Policies
This worksheet asks you to discover the sources of the information regarding the many policies, procedures, and schedules of the school.

Worksheet 1 - 6 School Equipment
This worksheet calls on you to identify the processes to access school equipment.

Worksheet 1 - 7 Noninstructional Duties
This worksheet will acquaint you with other expectations of your time in school, such as lunchroom or bulletin board duties.

Worksheet 1 - 8 Personnel Policies
This worksheet informs you of the personnel policies in place in your school.

Worksheet 1 - 9 Public Resources
This worksheet informs you of the educational resources beyond the school community.

Worksheet 1 - 10 School Places
This worksheet asks you to locate the facilities and identify the personnel of the school and parish.

Worksheet 1 - 11 The Local Community
This worksheet will acquaint you with the parish neighborhoods.

Worksheet 1 - 1
Orientation to School Personnel

Directions: Please record the names of key personnel you will need to interact with at this school.

Administrators:

    Pastor   _____

    Associate Pastor   _____

    Associate Pastor   _____

    Principal   _____

    Assistant Principal   _____

Office Staff:

    Administrative Assistant   _____

    Office Assistant   _____

Support Personnel:

    Director of Religious Education   _____

    Math Coordinator   _____

    Language Arts Coordinator   _____

    Science Coordinator   _____

    Social Studies Coordinator   _____

    Physical Education Coordinator   _____

    Fine Arts Coordinator   _____

    Resource Specialist   _____

    Guidance Counselor   _____

Plant Staff:

    Business Manager   _____

    Maintenance   _____

    Custodian   _____

_____   _____   _____   _____

New Teacher   Buddy Teacher   Principal   Date

Worksheet 1 - 2
School Resources

Directions: Beyond the immediate instructional and office staff, the new teacher needs to know other members of the school community. Please identify the following significant persons of the school community.

School Board President	_____
School Board Vice President	_____
School Board Member	_____
School Board Member	_____
School Board Member	_____
School Board Member	_____
Home & School Association President	_____
Home & School Association Vice President	_____
Home & School Association Secretary	_____
Home & School Association Treasurer	_____
Home & School Association Board Member	_____
Home & School Association Board Member	_____
Hot Lunch Manager	_____
Hot Lunch Assistant	_____
Hot Lunch Assistant	_____
Yard Duty Assistant	_____
Yard Duty Assistant	_____
Yard Duty Assistant	_____
School Nurse	_____
Lunch Time Nurse	_____
Health Chairperson	_____
Fundraising Chairperson	_____

_____   _____   _____   _____
New Teacher   Buddy Teacher   Principal   Date

Worksheet 1 - 3
Diocesan Resource Personnel

Directions: As a member of the larger Catholic school community, the arch/diocese, a teacher should be aware of the personnel that provide assistance at that level. Please identify the following individuals.

Superintendent of Schools _____

Assistant Superintendent _____

Assistant Superintendent _____

Administrative Assistant _____

Placement Coordinator _____

Insurance Coordinator _____

Arch/Diocesan School
    Board President _____

Arch/Diocesan School Board
    Secretary _____

Others

_____ _____

_____ _____

_____ _____

_____ _____

_____

_____ _____ _____ _____
New Teacher Buddy Teacher Principal Date

Worksheet 1 - 4
Paper Work

Directions: The new teacher needs to be aware of the proper procedures for processing paper work. This worksheet will serve as a validation that this knowledge has been attained. Please initial and date as you discover the information about each item. Your buddy teacher can help you with this.

Item	**Initial**	**Date**

Organizing the register:
    Documenting tardies _____ _____
    Documenting absences _____ _____
    Parents' notes _____ _____

Cumulative records:
    Location _____ _____
    Inclusions _____ _____
    Deadlines _____ _____

Parental Communication:
    Progress reports _____ _____
    Report cards _____ _____
    Parent-teacher conferences _____ _____
    Routine communications _____ _____
    Special conferences _____ _____
    Field trip permission forms _____ _____

Communication with Principal:
    Scheduled conferences _____ _____
    Special conferences _____ _____
    Lesson plans _____ _____
    Substitute folder _____ _____
    Materials/repair requests _____ _____
    Field trip requests _____ _____
    Student referrals _____ _____

Communication with Staff:
    Faculty meetings _____ _____
    Bulletin boards _____ _____
    Faculty bulletins _____ _____

_____   _____   _____   _____
New Teacher   Buddy Teacher   Principal   Date

Worksheet 1 - 5
Schedules and Policies

Directions: The efficient functioning of the school requires that the new teacher understand and implement established policies, procedures, and schedules. Please indicate below the date and source of your information regarding each of the items.

Policies, Procedures Schedules & information	Initial/date	Source
Teacher job description	_____	_____
Student referral process	_____	_____
Yearly calendar	_____	_____
Monthly calendar	_____	_____
Daily class schedule	_____	_____
Special day schedule	_____	_____
Mass/assembly schedule	_____	_____
School behavior policy	_____	_____
Class behavior policy	_____	_____
Fire drill policy/procedure	_____	_____
Disaster policy/procedure	_____	_____
Emergency policy/procedure	_____	_____
Maintenance/custodial request	_____	_____

_____   _____   _____   _____
New Teacher   Buddy Teacher   Principal   Date

Worksheet 1 - 6
School Equipment

Directions: The new teacher needs to know where equipment and supplies are located and how to access them. Identify the process to access the items noted below and state the date when this information was acquired.

Item	Process	Date
Computers/printers	_____	_____
Film strip projectors	_____	_____
Slide projectors	_____	_____
Video player	_____	_____
Video camera	_____	_____
Audio recorders	_____	_____
Playground equipment	_____	_____
Overhead projector	_____	_____
Medical supplies	_____	_____
_____	_____	_____
_____	_____	_____
_____	_____	_____
_____	_____	_____

_____ _____ _____ _____
New Teacher   Buddy Teacher   Principal   Date

Worksheet 1 - 7
Noninstructional Duties

Directions: Although much of your time and energy will be devoted toward instructional activities, you should be aware of the non-instructional duties of faculty members at your school. Initial and date each item once you have discussed it with your principal and buddy teacher. It is important to add any responsibility not identified below that is an expectation for teachers at your school.

Item	Initial	Date
Yard and/or lunchtime supervisor	_____	_____
Faculty room duty	_____	_____
School bulletin board responsibility	_____	_____
Faculty meeting prayer	_____	_____
Subject area chairperson	_____	_____
Student council moderator/advisor	_____	_____
Athletic team coach	_____	_____
Mission moderator	_____	_____
Catholic Schools Week advisor	_____	_____
Parent club representative	_____	_____
Other_____	_____	_____
_____	_____	_____
_____	_____	_____

_____   _____   _____   _____
New Teacher   Buddy Teacher   Principal   Date

Worksheet 1 - 8
Personnel Policies

Directions: It is important for the new teacher to understand the objective rules of the workplace. To do this you will need to consult primary sources for information. These sources should include your diocesan personnel handbook, your local school personnel handbook, and any pertinent laws affecting private schools. Initial and date each issue you have discussed with your principal and buddy teacher. Please add other issues pertinent to your school that are not mentioned here.

Policy	**Initial**	**Date**
Salary	_____	_____
Health benefits	_____	_____
Sick leave	_____	_____
Personal days	_____	_____
Pension	_____	_____
Probation/post probationary status	_____	_____
Grievance procedures	_____	_____
Professional growth requirements	_____	_____
Health requirements	_____	_____
Child abuse clearance	_____	_____
Other_____	_____	_____
_____	_____	_____
_____	_____	_____
_____	_____	_____
_____	_____	_____

_____   _____   _____   _____
New Teacher   Buddy Teacher   Principal   Date

Worksheet 1 - 9
Public Resources

Directions: Local public resources may be able to give you much support. List the names of the following individuals and the date that you identified them.

District or County Offices of Education:

	Name	**Date**
Superintendent of Government Schools	_____	_____
Curriculum Specialists	_____	_____
Technology Specialists	_____	_____
Others	_____	_____
	_____	_____

Public Resources:

	Name	Date
Public Libraries	_____	_____
	_____	_____
Museums	_____	_____
	_____	_____
Others		
_____	_____	_____
_____	_____	_____
_____	_____	_____
_____	_____	_____

_____   _____   _____   _____
New Teacher   Buddy Teacher   Principal   Date

Worksheet 1 - 10
School Places

Directions: The new teacher needs to be familiar with the school and parish facilities. Indicate with date and initials when you have visited the following places.

Place	Date	Initial
School offices	_____	_____
Faculty room	_____	_____
Classrooms (K-8)	_____	_____
School hall	_____	_____
Library	_____	_____
Science laboratory	_____	_____
Computer laboratory	_____	_____
Bathrooms (lower and upper grades)	_____	_____
Playground areas	_____	_____
Store room	_____	_____
Physical education equipment room	_____	_____
CCD office and classrooms	_____	_____
Extended care office	_____	_____
Preschool	_____	_____
Kitchen for hot lunch	_____	_____
Janitor's supply closet	_____	_____
Parish center	_____	_____
Business manager's office	_____	_____
Parish rectory	_____	_____
Convent	_____	_____
Church	_____	_____
Sacristy	_____	_____
_____	_____	_____
_____	_____	_____

Obtain a plant/facilities map from the principal, and label as many of the identified places as you can. Insert the map into the orientation booklet.

_____   _____   _____   _____
New Teacher   Buddy Teacher   Principal   Date

Worksheet 1 - 11
The Local Community

Directions: To be able to effectively minister to the children in a class a teacher should have a realistic understanding of the students' local community and culture. Indicate with date and initials when you have studied the following factors and discussed them with your principal and buddy teacher.

Factors	Initial	Date
Ethnic diversity of population	_____	_____
Socioeconomic levels	_____	_____
Cultural identity (past/present)	_____	_____
Geographic distinctions	_____	_____
Educational priority	_____	_____
Community profile (e.g. business/commercial/residential	_____	_____
	_____	_____
Active civic groups	_____	_____
Adult issues	_____	_____
Youth issues	_____	_____
Other		
_____	_____	_____
_____	_____	_____
_____	_____	_____

_____ _____ _____ _____
New Teacher Buddy Teacher Principal Date

2
Creating the Classroom Climate

Creating the Classroom Climate

One of the factors that consistently surfaces in the literature regarding effective schools is the need for a climate that is conducive to learning. Now when this factor is cited it typically refers to the total school climate. However, for such a supportive climate to pervade the entire school, a similar atmosphere must be present in each classroom.

This is one of the areas in which you, the new teacher, can feel a certain degree of success early on in the year. If it is going to come about, however, it won't happen by accident. You will need coaching and support both in regard to general principles of classroom climate and, in particular, to the characteristics of the students you will be educating this year.

The physical environment of your classroom, classroom management and procedures will be addressed in the upcoming pages. These areas are very crucial ones for you. These topics call for careful review and detailed discussion. As you assimilate this important information, you will rely on the experience and expertise of your buddy teacher and principal to assist you in creating a positive classroom setting. While you need freedom to create a personal teaching style and a supportive classroom atmosphere, these must be based on sound learning principles.

Not to be overlooked in the preparation of the classroom is the consideration of the students. Beyond the physical makeup of the room and the procedures for getting things done, you are preparing to interact and direct the students. How this is done can drastically affect the climate of the classroom. Thoughtful discussions between the buddy teacher and you or between the principal and you will lead you to create a supportive environment as you interact with the students.

The following pages provide opportunities for you to create a positive learning environment based on thoughtful reflection.

This chapter offers the following worksheets to assist you.

Worksheet 2 - 1 Philosophy
Catholic schools have a unique philosophy. This philosophy is best expressed in several key documents. This worksheet will direct you to some of these.

Worksheet 2 - 2 Religious Practices
An important part of a Catholic school is its religious practices. This worksheet lists these for you.

Worksheet 2 - 3 The Classroom
This worksheet provides a reference point for you, the new teacher, as you begin to organize the classroom.

Worksheet 2 - 4 Classroom Management
This worksheet elicits ideas from you that will promote the building of a positive climate in the classroom.

Worksheet 2 - 5 Classroom Procedures
This worksheet asks you to identify classroom operating procedures that will contribute to an orderly environment.

Worksheet 2 - 6 Classroom Energy
This worksheet calls for you to illustrate ways that you can direct the energy of the students within your classroom.

Worksheet 2 - 7 The First Day of School
This worksheet calls on you to envision the first day of school through the eyes of a student, so as to prepare more thoughtfully for the students.

Worksheet 2 - 1
Philosophy

Directions: All activities at the local school should reflect a Catholic philosophy of education. The new teacher needs to be familiar with this philosophy from a variety of perspectives—local, regional, and national. Indicate with date and initials when you have reviewed the following documents and discussed them with your principal and buddy teacher.

Document	Date	Initial
To Teach as Jesus Did	_____	_____
Religious Dimensions of Education in a Catholic School	_____	_____
National Congress on Catholic Schools for the 21st Century: Executive Summary	_____	_____
The National Catechetical Directory	_____	_____
The diocesan philosophy of education	_____	_____
The local school's philosophy of education	_____	_____
New teacher's philosophy of education	_____	_____
NCEA Code of Ethics for the Catholic School Teacher	_____	_____
Other_____	_____	_____
_____	_____	_____
_____	_____	_____
_____	_____	_____

_____   _____   _____   _____
New Teacher   Buddy Teacher   Principal   Date

Worksheet 2 - 2
Religious Practices

Directions: The religious climate of the school can be greatly supported through religious practices employed by the school. The new teacher needs to be familiar with the policy of the school with respect to religious practices. Indicate with date and initials when you have discussed the following religious practices which may take place at the local school. Please add items that are not mentioned, but are part of the school's program.

Practice	**Date**	**Initial**
Class/school prayer	_____	_____
Prayer before meals	_____	_____
Prayer before/after classes	_____	_____
Class/school liturgies	_____	_____
Class/school Penance services	_____	_____
October devotions	_____	_____
Observance of holydays of obligation	_____	_____
Advent devotions	_____	_____
Christmas celebrations	_____	_____
Lenten devotions	_____	_____
Easter celebrations	_____	_____
Feast days	_____	_____
May crowning	_____	_____
Other		
_____	_____	_____
_____	_____	_____
_____	_____	_____
_____	_____	_____

_____   _____   _____   _____
New Teacher   Buddy Teacher   Principal   Date

Worksheet 2 - 3
The Classroom

Directions: The following is a check list for you to consider while preparing your classroom. Please respond to these questions and be prepared to discuss how they will affect the climate of your classroom.

Classroom Furniture:

How many student chairs and desks are in the room? _____

Are they arranged to facilitate a safe traffic pattern? _____

How many work tables are in the room? _____

Where are the learning centers? _____

Where is the teacher's desk? _____

What storage exists for the teacher? _____

Books/Learning Materials:

Is there an inventory of textbooks and supplemental books? _____

What reference books are in the classroom? _____

How many computers are in the classroom? _____

Does the classroom have computer programs? _____

Bulletin Boards:

How many bulletin boards are in the room? _____

What will be the focus of each? _____

How often will they be changed? _____

Who will change them? _____

Environmental control:

Does the room have a seating chart? _____

Are the discipline rules posted? _____

Are emergency procedures posted? _____

What things can be added to make the room attractive (plants, fish tank, pictures, etc.)? _____

Is the schedule for classroom "helpers" published? _____

Is a supply list available? _____

After reviewing these items, draw/sketch your classroom on the back of this sheet, indicating as many of the identified components as possible.

_____   _____   _____   _____
New Teacher   Buddy Teacher   Principal   Date

draw/sketch your classroom on this sheet, indicating as many of the identified components as possible.

Worksheet 2 - 4
Classroom Management

Directions: Please respond to the following statements which will serve as subject matter for discussions regarding basic elements of classroom management.

How do you plan to build a faith community within the classroom?
_____
_____
_____

How do you plan to build trust and self-esteem?
_____
_____
_____

How do you plan to set rules and consequences (positive and negative)?
_____
_____
_____

How do you plan to enforce rules?
_____
_____
_____

What incentives and rewards do you plan to use?
_____
_____
_____

How do you plan to teach problem solving strategies?
_____
_____
_____

_____   _____   _____   _____
New Teacher   Buddy Teacher   Principal   Date

Worksheet 2 - 5
Classroom Procedures

Directions: Basic classroom procedures can take a great deal of time and energy, and reduce the time available for instruction and learning. Talk to experienced teachers to discover how they manage these kinds of required activities and save themselves both time and energy. Take notes and be ready to discuss how you will handle these in your classroom.

Taking attendance:_____
_____
_____

Special announcements:_____
_____
_____

Collecting materials for the office: _____
_____
_____

Correcting homework or classwork:_____
_____
_____

Collecting/recording homework:_____
_____
_____

Passing out/collecting supplies:_____
_____
_____

Others:_____
_____
_____

_____   _____   _____   _____
New Teacher   Buddy Teacher   Principal   Date

Worksheet 2 - 6
Classroom Energy

Directions: Identify activities that you could use to quiet students and focus their attention. Consult other teachers for further ideas.

1. _____
   _____
   _____

2. _____
   _____
   _____

3. _____
   _____
   _____

4. _____
   _____
   _____

5. _____
   _____
   _____

Directions: Identify activities that you could use to energize, motivate students. Consult other teachers for further ideas.

1. _____
   _____
   _____

2. _____
   _____
   _____

3. _____
   _____
   _____

4. _____
   _____
   _____

_____   _____   _____   _____
New Teacher   Buddy Teacher   Principal   Date

Worksheet 2 - 7
The First Day of School

Directions: In *Educational Leadership*, D. Brooks presented the article "The First Day of School". He listed seven things students desperately want to know on the first day of school. These questions also apply to the new student at any time of the year. You need to plan activities to address these issues.

Write your plan below.

1. Am I in the right room ?
   _____
   _____

2. Where am I supposed to sit ?
   _____
   _____

3. What are the rules of this teacher ?
   _____
   _____

4. How will I be graded ?
   _____
   _____

5. What will I be doing ?
   _____
   _____

6. Who is the teacher as a person ?
   _____
   _____

7. Will the teacher be interested in me as a person ?
   _____
   _____

_____   _____   _____   _____
New Teacher   Buddy Teacher   Principal   Date

3

Planning Meaningful Lessons

Planning Meaningful Lessons

Essential for your success as a new teacher in this school, and for all teachers everywhere, is the ability to provide meaningful learning opportunities for the students. You probably have finished a credential/certificate program, or come with experience in the classroom, but even with a background in the delivery of instruction, you will find helpful discussions and conversations with experienced teachers regarding the lessons that will be presented in your new school.

This chapter first presents for you an outline for the construction of a lesson plan. This is not to be considered the definitive lesson plan; rather, it is a starting point that will lead to meaningful discussion, purposeful lesson planning, effective lessons, and improved learning.

Six-Step Lesson Plan

Step 1: The Anticipatory Set
    1.1   Teacher focuses the student
    1.2   Teacher states the learning objective
    1.3   Teacher establishes the purpose for the lesson
    1.4   Teacher establishes transfer from past learning, if appropriate

Step 2: Instruction
    2.1   Teacher pre-tests the students, if necessary, to identify students who may have problems acquiring the new skill or information

    2.2   Teacher presents the new information or skill

    2.3   Teacher models for the students the desired response

    2.4   Teacher checks each child's comprehension of the objective

Step 3: Guided Practice
    3.1   Students practice with teacher guidance

    3.2   Students demonstrate the required behavior of the objective.

    3.3   Teacher provides feedback to the students

    3.4   Teacher reteaches skill or concept to those needing more assistance

Step 4: Evaluating Performance
    4.1   Students demonstrate desired behavior without teacher intervention

Step 5: Independent Practice
- 5.1 Students have opportunity for continued practice to attain competency
- 5.2 Teacher begins with mass practice and then moves to distributed practice
- 5.3 Teacher returns the results of the practice to the students as soon as possible

Step 6: Follow Up
- 6.1 Teacher provides follow up exercises for students
- 6.2 Teacher applies concept or skill to daily living
- 6.3 Teacher may use the content of the instruction to help students to deepen their understanding and acceptance of a Christian value
- 6.4 Students discover use of knowledge or skill in their own lives
- 6.5 Students make connections of new skill or knowledge to information they already possess

Within each lesson, you will provide a variety of instructional strategies to enable students to acquire the desired learning. The following list is composed of possible instructional strategies that can be used in the construction of lesson plans. This is not meant to be an exhaustive list, but rather one for reference, and one that can be expanded throughout the year.

Instructional Strategies

Lecture: direct instruction, teacher gives an oral presentation

advantages
- presentation to large groups
- develops listening skills

disadvantages
- one-way communication process
- students in passive role
- no immediate check on understanding

Discussion: sharing of information by teacher and students to clarify a question/topic or solve a problem

advantages
- students play an active role
- encourages organization of facts to address question/topic
- promotes critical questions

disadvantages
- can be difficult to manage and unpredictable
- facilitation skills needed by director of discussion

Independent study: individual students study assigned and approved topics

> *advantages*
>> allows in-depth study in area of interest or need
>> can be used in all curricular areas
>
> *disadvantages*
>> little to no social interaction of students
>> independent work and/or research skills needed

Group work: a group of students organized for study on a particular project

> *advantages*
>> active participation in the learning process
>> allows for in-depth study in area of interest or need
>
> *disadvantages*
>> group skills can aid or deter achieving group goal
>> independent work and/or research skills needed

Hands on activities: students have first-hand experience with topic of study through field trips, manipulatives, use of technology, experiments, etc.

> *advantages*
>> direct student involvement and possible immediate feedback
>> often a multi-sensory experience
>
> *disadvantages*
>> requires teacher expertise/knowledge in area of project
>> planning time can be extensive

Simulation: students role play for the purpose of gaining greater insight and understanding of a situation

> *advantages*
>> can be motivating experience
>> promotes experimentation within the role
>> can provide indepth insight
>
> *disadvantages*
>> requires the use of imagination
>> can be time consuming

If there are other rubrics for delivery of instruction at this particular school, they should be included in discussion. The principal and/or buddy teacher may want to present a lesson for you, the new teacher, illustrating the predominant manner for the delivery of instruction at this school. The material that is in this chapter can then be used for comparative analysis. Also, you, yourself, may have material to share regarding the design and delivery of instruction based on your training and/or experience. Please do not hesitate to share this with your colleagues.

A Strategy for Incorporating a Value into a Lesson

While the following strategy has eight steps to it, you should realize that this process can and should be gone over very quickly. In addition some of the steps may be part of the general lesson. You should recall that the length of the value component of the lesson is not the important feature in deepening values in students. Students will internalize values when they have frequent exposure to them and this exposure is related to real life experiences. This strategy includes these steps.

1. The teacher selects the content to be learned, determines the skill students will need to acquire the content, and decides if the content provides an opportunity for a discussion of a Christian value. Not every lesson must have a value component to it.

2. The teacher through informal processes discovers if students have the skill to acquire the content.

3. The students apply the skill and discover the content. The teacher provides individual assistance to those students having problems.

4. Through questioning, the teacher leads the students to discover the Christian value in the content.

5. The teacher recalls a Christian dimension to the value by referring to an event in the life of Jesus, a saying of Jesus, the life of a saint, or a quotation from a church document that exemplifies the value.

6. Students reflect on how they have lived out the value in their lives.

7. Students share their reflections in their journals, in small groups, or to the entire class.

8. The teacher challenges the students to do something in the near future that requires them to act motivated by the value.

The following worksheets are for you, the principal and buddy teacher to use in the discussion of planning and implementing instructional activities within the classroom.

Worksheet 3 - 1 Lesson Design Planning Sheet
This first worksheet can be used in the design of the lesson plan by you in collaboration with the principal or buddy teacher.

Worksheet 3 - 2 Lesson Plan Review
This worksheet may be used by you with the principal and/or buddy teacher to review a lesson plan created by yourself.

Worksheet 3 - 3 Curriculum
The curriculum is your teaching guide. Become familiar with the books mentioned on this worksheet.

Worksheet 3 - 1
Lesson Design Planning Sheet

Teacher _____ Support Person _____

Subject/Class _____ Date _____

Lesson Objective:

Step 1 - The Anticipatory Set

Step 2 - Instruction

Step 3 - Guided Practice

Step 4 - Evaluating Performance

Step 5 - Independent Practice

Step 6 - Follow Up

_____ _____   _____   _____
New Teacher   Buddy Teacher   Principal   Date

Worksheet 3 - 2
Lesson Plan Review

1. Objective

   What is the objective for this lesson?

2. Activities

   What activities will be used to attain this objective?

3. Design

   How will the activities be structured to achieve the objective? Items for consideration will include pacing, time available, and difficulty of objectives for this group.

4. Assessment

   How will you determine if the objectives are achieved?

5. Follow up

   What is the next step?

_____   _____   _____   _____
New Teacher   Buddy Teacher   Principal   Date

Worksheet 3 - 3
Curriculum

Directions: The new teacher should rely on the support of existing documents to provide guidance and direction as lesson plans and instructional units are developed. Please consult the following documents and discuss them with your principal and buddy teacher for clarity. Indicate with date and initials that you have discussed each item.

Document	Date	Initials
Diocesan Curriculum Guidelines	_____	_____
State framework for instruction in curriculum areas	_____	_____
Local school curriculum guidelines	_____	_____
Existing instructional units	_____	_____
Other_____	_____	_____
_____	_____	_____
_____	_____	_____
_____	_____	_____

_____ _____   _____   _____
New Teacher   Buddy Teacher   Principal   Date

4 *Support*

Support

This chapter provides you, the new teacher, with an opportunity to reflect on the people and the various learning experiences that can provide support to you. The intent of this new teacher orientation program is to promote your success as a teacher. In a very real sense, this process involves you with as many people as possible in the Catholic school community in order to show you the great support that you have here. You should recall, however, that your primary supporters are your buddy teacher and the principal. These are the two people with whom to share problems, request guidance and ask feedback. You should never hesitate to speak to them and ask their advice. Your principal is more than just your boss; your principal is the leader of this community that wants to enable you to become a most effective educator. The success of the school depends on the success of each teacher in every classroom. Everyone wants to help you become very successful.

Worksheet 4 - 1 Faculty Who Can Help
This worksheet asks you, the new teacher, to become more acquainted with the faculty and their capabilities to help you.

Worksheet 4 - 2 Plan for Success
This reflective sheet you will complete after you have had an opportunity to experience the day-to-day tasks of teaching . You are to ask yourself, "What is the one thing that would make my teaching life easier?" Having identified this aspect of the teaching situation, you now develop a plan to overcome this obstacle.

Worksheet 4 - 3 Plan for Success: Action Plan
This form helps you to become very concrete in setting short-term objectives for yourself and establishing a realistic plan to achieve them.

Worksheet 4 - 1
Faculty Who Can Help

Directions: You have available to you a list of all the teachers, teacher assistants, and staff. Use this page as a help to get to know them. On the line provided ask them to sign your book and indicate one area where they can provide assistance, support, or guidance.

Name	How I can help!
_____	_____
_____	_____
_____	_____
_____	_____
_____	_____
_____	_____
_____	_____
_____	_____
_____	_____
_____	_____
_____	_____
_____	_____
_____	_____
_____	_____
_____	_____
_____	_____

_____   _____   _____   _____
New Teacher   Buddy Teacher   Principal   Date

Worksheet 4 - 2
Plan for Success

My greatest challenge
    Identify that one specific thing, student, task, etc. that is of greatest concern to you.

The ideal
    What would be the ideal state/resolution of this situation ?

The response
    With your principal or buddy teacher, work out possible responses/solutions to the situation identified.

Timetable
    Again working with the principal and/or buddy teacher, identify a realistic timeline for implementation your plan. Brainstorm ideas and then complete the next worksheet.

_____   _____   _____   _____
New Teacher   Buddy Teacher   Principal   Date

Worksheet 4 - 3
Plan for Success: Action Plan

Below is a form/template to help you organize your action plan. Develop this with the aid of your buddy teacher and principal based on your answers to the previous questions. Use one sheet for each activity. The components of the plan are:

Objective -   What needs to be changed?

Activity -   What specific action will help to achieve this change?

Person -   Who will facilitate the accomplishment of this action?

Timeline -   When does each activity need to be accomplished?

Success -   What shows this has helped to achieve the objective?

Objective:

Activity:

Person responsible:

Timeline:

Success:

_____   _____   _____   _____
New Teacher   Buddy Teacher   Principal   Date

5

Teacher's Professional Journal

Teacher's Professional Journal

This chapter provides a form on the next page that is a template for entries into your professional journal. These entries are to be kept by you, the new teacher, with input from any support people you feel would be appropriate.

You may use the form exactly as is, or may make some adaption to it before completing it. The form may be duplicated or kept on a computer. Another possibility is that you use the items noted on the form as guides and keep a journal in a notebook. Some additional papers have been provided so you may use this bok as your journal.

The important thing is that you, as a new teacher, keep a reflective professional journal as a record and reference of the professional dialogue between you and those who play a part in your orientation. This journal will serve a valuable resource in reviewing the progress made during the period of orientation.

Worksheet 5 - 1
Teacher's Professional Journal

Date _____

Participants   Topics

_____   _____

_____   _____

_____   _____

Notes/Summary

Action Items

_____   _____   _____   _____
New Teacher   Buddy Teacher   Principal   Date

Worksheet 5 - 1
Teacher's Professional Journal

Date _____

Participants   Topics

_____   _____

_____   _____

_____   _____

Notes/Summary

Action Items

_____   _____   _____   _____
New Teacher   Buddy Teacher   Principal   Date

Worksheet 5 - 1
Teacher's Professional Journal

Date _____

Participants　　　　　　　　　　　　　　Topics

_____　　　_____

_____　　　_____

_____　　　_____

Notes/Summary

Action Items

_____　　_____　　　_____　　_____
New Teacher　　　Buddy Teacher　　　　Principal　　　　　Date

Worksheet 5 - 1
Teacher's Professional Journal

Date _____

Participants   Topics

_____   _____

_____   _____

_____   _____

Notes/Summary

Action Items

_____   _____   _____   _____
New Teacher   Buddy Teacher   Principal   Date

Worksheet 5 - 1
Teacher's Professional Journal

Date _____

Participants   Topics

_____   _____

_____   _____

_____   _____

Notes/Summary

Action Items

_____   _____   _____   _____
New Teacher   Buddy Teacher   Principal   Date

Worksheet 5 - 1
Teacher's Professional Journal

Date _____

Participants   Topics

_____   _____

_____   _____

_____   _____

Notes/Summary

Action Items

_____   _____   _____   _____
New Teacher   Buddy Teacher   Principal   Date

Worksheet 5 - 1
Teacher's Professional Journal

Date _____

Participants   Topics

_____   _____

_____   _____

_____   _____

Notes/Summary

Action Items

_____   _____   _____   _____
New Teacher   Buddy Teacher   Principal   Date

Computer Specifications

This computer disk contains all of the worksheets that appear in the text of the book. The first thing the principal should do is make a backup disk and store it in a safe place.

The disk is provided to enable the principal to customize the forms to the specifics of his/her school. The program used for the forms is MicroSoft Works 3.0 which can be run on a Macintosh computer; the principal may also choose an IBM WordPerfect 5.1 version. Four megabytes of random access memory (RAM) will normally be sufficient to run the program.

In addition to customizing and reprinting the forms, the computer disk provides another option. The computer disk can be utilized to document the orientation entirely on the computer. If you don't need another piece of paper in your life, you can fill in the forms on the computer by highlighting the line that you would like to input information; for the Macintosh computer, select the underline function from the Style option on the menu bar; and then, merely type in your information.

The computer disk is provided as an attempt to meet the needs and/or preferences of the principals and teachers who will be using this program. Take advantage of those options that you are comfortable using.